CHUPACABRAS!

STEVEN ROBERTS

PowerKiDS
press.

New York

Published in 2013 by The Rosen Publishing Group, Inc.
29 East 21st Street, New York, NY 10010

First Edition

Editor: Joanne Randolph
Book Design: Planman Technologies
Illustrations: Planman Technologies

Library of Congress Cataloging-in-Publication Data

Roberts, Steven.
 Chupacabras! / by Steven Roberts. —1st ed.
     p. cm. — (Jr. graphic monster stories)
 Includes index.
 ISBN 978-1-4488-7902-1 (library binding) — ISBN 978-1-4488-8002-7 (pbk.) — ISBN 978-1-4488-8008-9 (6-pack)
 1. Chupacabras--Juvenile literature. I. Title.
 QL89.2.C57R63 2013
 001.944—dc23

                             2012004337

Manufactured in the United States of America

CPSIA Compliance Information: Batch # SW12PK: For Further Information contact Rosen Publishing, New York, New York at 1-800-237-9932

Contents

Main Characters

Evelyn Esbry (c. 2000s) **Attacked** by a chupacabra in her own backyard in April 2000 near Calama, Chile.

Devin Mcanally (c. 2000s) Rancher near San Antonio, Texas, who killed a creature called the Elmendorf **Beast** in 2004 that was thought to be a chupacabra.

Osvaldo Rosado (c. 1990s) Mechanic who fought off a sudden, **savage** attack by a chupacabra near Guánica, Puerto Rico, in 1995.

Chupacabra Facts

- Most people who claim to have seen a chupacabra describe the beast as being about 4 feet (1.2 m) tall with a hunched back and **quills** running down its spine. It looks like a **reptile** with gray-green, scaly skin and a long tail. They say it walks on its hind legs and has arms with sharp **claws** for tearing flesh. The chupacabra is said to have large teeth with **fangs** for sucking blood from animals. It is very quick on its feet and hard to catch. Some observers have described it as being able to walk across rooftops easily or scale steep cliffs.

- For many **generations**, natives of the South American rain forest have told stories of a "mosquito man" that sucks the blood from its animal victims. It is thought to be the same creature as the chupacabra.

- Some people are convinced that the chupacabra is an **alien**. They think it may have been mistakenly left on Earth by a visiting alien spaceship.

Chupacabras!

ETHAN WAS VISITING HIS FRIEND DIEGO.

BY THE WAY, I GOT A NEW PET. DO YOU WANT TO SEE HIM?

SURE.

CHUPACABRA! CHUPACABRA!

CHUPACABRA? WHAT KIND OF A NAME IS THAT?

YOU HAVE NEVER HEARD OF A CHUPACABRA?

NO. WHAT IS IT?

"THE CHUPACABRA IS A CREATURE THAT SUCKS THE BLOOD OUT OF ANIMALS AND SOMETIMES ATTACKS PEOPLE.

"STORIES OF THE CHUPACABRA GO BACK AS FAR AS THE 1950S. THERE HAVE BEEN SIGHTINGS OF CHUPACABRAS IN THE UNITED STATES, MEXICO, PUERTO RICO, AND SOUTH AMERICA.

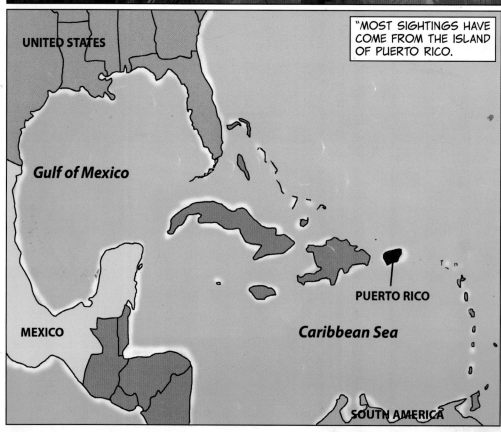

"MOST SIGHTINGS HAVE COME FROM THE ISLAND OF PUERTO RICO.

UNITED STATES

Gulf of Mexico

MEXICO

Caribbean Sea

PUERTO RICO

SOUTH AMERICA

"ONE NIGHT IN 1975, PEOPLE ALL ACROSS PUERTO RICO REPORTED SEEING STRANGE LIGHTS IN THE SKY.

"OVER THE NEXT FEW DAYS, FARMERS IN THE TOWN OF MOCA FOUND THAT MANY OF THEIR ANIMALS HAD BEEN KILLED."

MY ANIMALS ARE DEAD! I AM RUINED!

"POLICE INVESTIGATED THE KILLINGS."

DID YOU SEE OR HEAR ANYTHING?

NO. IT HAPPENED AT NIGHT.

"A **VETERINARIAN** EXAMINED THE ANIMALS AND FOUND SOMETHING THAT SURPRISED HIM."

THIS IS ODD.

"THE ANIMALS HAD **PUNCTURE** MARKS ON THEIR BODIES, AND ALL THE BLOOD HAD BEEN DRAINED FROM THEM."

"NEWS OF THE ATTACKS QUICKLY SPREAD. PEOPLE'S IMAGINATIONS RAN WILD."

THIS IS SOME KIND OF MONSTER!

IT COULD ATTACK OUR CHILDREN!

"SOME THOUGHT THE LIGHTS THEY HAD SEEN IN THE SKY A FEW DAYS BEFORE WERE SPACESHIPS. THEY SAID THE ATTACKS WERE THE WORK OF AN ALIEN ANIMAL THE SPACESHIPS HAD BROUGHT TO EARTH."

"MANY THOUGHT THE ANIMAL DEATHS WERE THE WORK OF A BLOOD-SUCKING BEAST KNOWN AS THE MOCA **VAMPIRE**."

NOBODY ACTUALLY SAW THE CREATURE. THEN IN 1995, THERE WERE MORE ATTACKS IN PUERTO RICO.

"HUNDREDS OF GOATS, CHICKENS, SHEEP, AND OTHER ANIMALS WERE KILLED. MANY OF THESE KILLINGS TOOK PLACE NEAR THE CITY OF CANÓVANAS."

"LIKE BEFORE, THE ANIMALS HAD FANG MARKS ON THEIR NECKS, AND ALL THE BLOOD WAS DRAINED FROM THEIR BODIES."

IT IS THE SAME CREATURE!

"FINALLY A GROUP OF TOWNSPEOPLE SAW THE TERRIBLE CREATURE AS IT WAS ABOUT TO ATTACK SOME GOATS."

GET AWAY, BEAST!

LEAVE THE ANIMALS ALONE!

HISSS!

SNARL!

"THE TOWNSPEOPLE THREW ROCKS AT THE CREATURE AND CHASED IT AWAY."

GET OUT!

GO AWAY!

"IN THE TOWN OF GUÁNICA, PUERTO RICO, A MAN NAMED OSVALDO ROSADO WAS ATTACKED BY ONE OF THE CREATURES AND FOUGHT IT OFF."

SNARL!

AHHHHH!

STAY BACK!

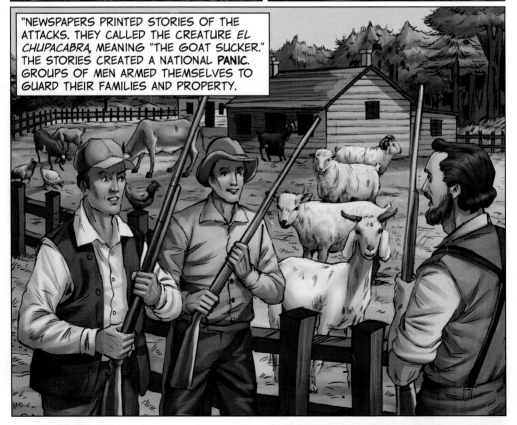

"NEWSPAPERS PRINTED STORIES OF THE ATTACKS. THEY CALLED THE CREATURE *EL CHUPACABRA,* MEANING "THE GOAT SUCKER." THE STORIES CREATED A NATIONAL **PANIC.** GROUPS OF MEN ARMED THEMSELVES TO GUARD THEIR FAMILIES AND PROPERTY."

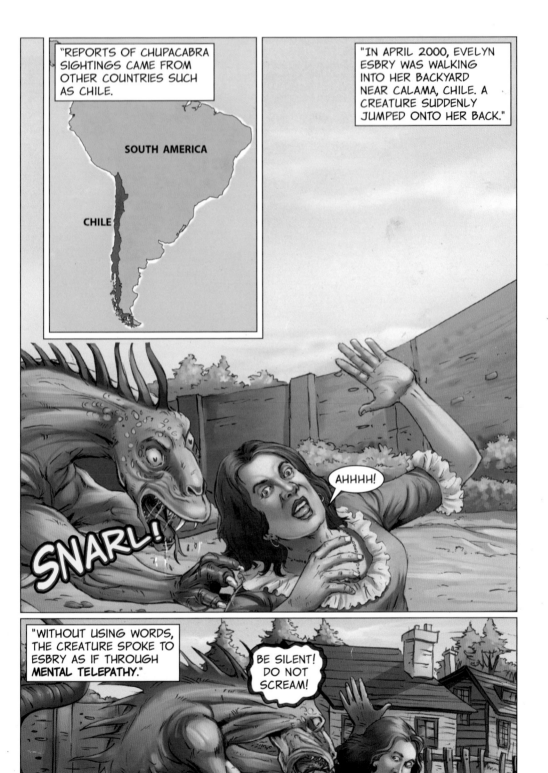

"REPORTS OF CHUPACABRA SIGHTINGS CAME FROM OTHER COUNTRIES SUCH AS CHILE.

SOUTH AMERICA

CHILE

"IN APRIL 2000, EVELYN ESBRY WAS WALKING INTO HER BACKYARD NEAR CALAMA, CHILE. A CREATURE SUDDENLY JUMPED ONTO HER BACK."

AHHHH!

SNARL!

"WITHOUT USING WORDS, THE CREATURE SPOKE TO ESBRY AS IF THROUGH MENTAL TELEPATHY."

BE SILENT! DO NOT SCREAM!

"IN MEXICO, A FARMER FOUGHT A CHUPACABRA THAT WAS ATTACKING HIS ANIMALS.

"THE CHUPACABRA JUMPED ONTO THE BARN ROOF AND THEN LEAPED TO THE GROUND AND RAN AWAY.

"IN JULY 2004, DEVIN MCANALLY, A RANCHER, KILLED A CREATURE ATTACKING HIS CHICKENS NEAR SAN ANTONIO, TEXAS."

"THE ANIMAL BECAME KNOWN AS THE ELMENDORF BEAST.

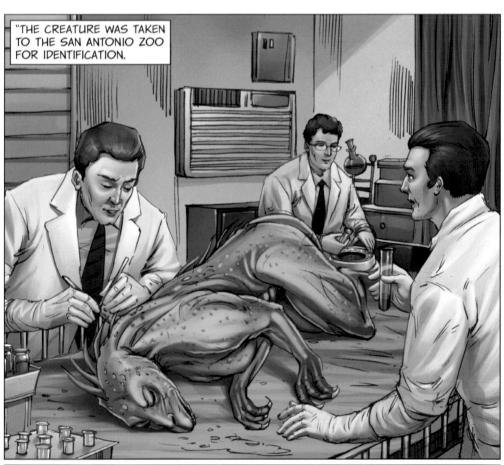

"THE CREATURE WAS TAKEN TO THE SAN ANTONIO ZOO FOR IDENTIFICATION.

"SCIENTISTS CONCLUDED THAT THE CREATURE WAS A COYOTE WITH A SEVERE CASE OF **MANGE**. MANGE IS A SKIN DISEASE THAT CAUSES AN ANIMAL'S FUR TO FALL OUT AND ITS SKIN TO SHRIVEL UP.

MANY PEOPLE ARE NOT CONVINCED THAT THIS SOLVED THE MYSTERY OF THE CHUPACABRA.

"SOME BELIEVE THE CREATURE IS THE PRODUCT OF A **GENETIC** EXPERIMENT BY THE US GOVERNMENT. THEY THINK IT ESCAPED FROM A LAB.

"SOME PEOPLE THINK THE CHUPACABRA IS AN UNKNOWN ANIMAL FROM AFRICA OR AUSTRALIA THAT CAME TO THE AMERICAS HIDDEN ON BOARD A SHIP.

"SIGHTINGS OF CHUPACABRAS STILL CONTINUE. THEY HAVE EVEN BEEN SEEN IN BIG CITIES LIKE MIAMI, NEW YORK, AND SAN DIEGO.

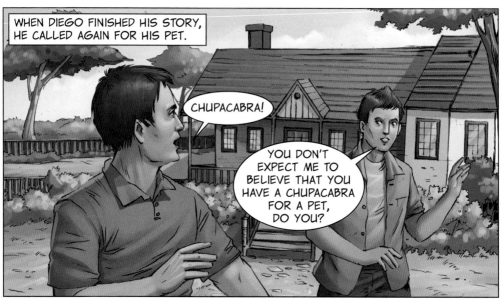

WHEN DIEGO FINISHED HIS STORY, HE CALLED AGAIN FOR HIS PET.

CHUPACABRA!

YOU DON'T EXPECT ME TO BELIEVE THAT YOU HAVE A CHUPACABRA FOR A PET, DO YOU?

YOU TELL ME. HERE HE COMES NOW.

AHHHH! WHAT IS IT?

More Chupacabra Stories

- **Attack on a Dog in Calama, Chile**
  In 2000, a young man was riding a bicycle past an alley. He heard a strange groan. Thinking someone needed help, he stopped and went into the alley. There he found a dead dog with a bloody neck. Hunched over the dog was a chupacabra. It looked up at him with red eyes and snarled. The creature picked up the dog and ran away with it down the alley.

- **Nightclub Incident in Maria Elena, Chile**
  One night in 2000, Carlos Silva heard pounding on the back screen door of his nightclub. David, one of his employees, went to the door to investigate, carrying a broomstick for protection. There he found a strange creature trying to break open the door. When another employee brought a bright flashlight to the back door, the creature jumped into a tree and fled across the rooftops. The creature was about 3 to 4 feet (1–1.2 m) tall with bright red eyes. It left a powerful smell near the back door. David became convinced it was a chupacabra.

- **The Grunch Road Chupacabra**
  Sightings of strange creatures are not uncommon on remote Grunch Road near New Orleans, Louisiana. Since the time Louisiana was first settled, many have seen what some locals think is a chupacabra living in this area. They call it the Grunch.

- **Dead Chupacabras near San Antonio**
  In 2007, Phylis Canion and her neighbors found the dead bodies of three strange creatures by the side of the road near her home about 80 miles (129 km) southeast of San Antonio, Texas. She saved the head of one of the creatures so it could be identified. She believes these were the animals that attacked her chickens and drained them of their blood. Many people believe these creatures were chupacabras.

Glossary

alien (AY-lee-un) A creature from outer space.

attacked (uh-TAKD) Tried to hurt someone or something.

beast (BEEST) An animal.

claws (KLAWZ) The sharp parts of an animal's feet.

fangs (FANGZ) Long, sharp teeth.

generations (jeh-nuh-RAY-shunz) Periods of time marked by all the people who are born in the same period.

genetic (jih-NEH-tik) Relating to the science that deals with the passing of features from parents to children.

mange (MAYNJ) An illness that causes all an animal's fur to fall out and its skin to get wrinkled.

mental telepathy (MEN-tul teh-LEH-puh-thee) Using the mind to speak to another or read his or her thoughts.

panic (PA-nik) A sudden feeling of fear.

puncture (PUNGK-cher) A hole.

quills (KWILZ) Large, stiff feathers.

reptile (REP-tyl) A cold-blooded animal with thin, dry pieces of skin called scales.

savage (SA-vij) Wild.

vampire (VAM-py-er) A dead person or creature from stories and folktales that sucks the blood of living people.

veterinarian (veh-tuh-ruh-NER-ee-un) A doctor who treats animals.

Index

Websites

Due to the changing nature of Internet links, PowerKids Press has
developed an online list of websites related to the subject of this
book. This site is updated regularly. Please use this link to access
the list:

www.powerkidslinks.com/mons/chup/